ABOUT ROB COUTEAU:

Positive reviews of Rob Couteau's books have appeared in the *Midwest Book Review*, *Publishers Weekly Select*, and Barney Rosset's *Evergreen Review*. In 1985 he won the North American Essay Award, a competition sponsored by the American Humanist Association. His work as a critic, interviewer, and social commentator has been featured in books such as *Gabriel Garcia Marquez's 'Love in the Time of Cholera'* by Thomas Fahy, *Conversations with Ray Bradbury* edited by Steven Aggelis, *Ghetto Images in Twentieth-Century American Literature* by Tyrone R. Simpson, and David Cohen's *Forgotten Millions*, a book about the homeless mentally ill. Over one-hundred selections of his poetry and prose have appeared in over forty-five periodicals. Couteau's interviews include conversations with Ray Bradbury, Pulitzer Prize-winning author Justin Kaplan, *Last Exit to Brooklyn* novelist Hubert Selby, Simon & Schuster editor Michael Korda, LSD discoverer Dr. Albert Hofmann, Picasso's model and muse Sylvette David, Nabokov biographer Robert Roper, music producer Danny Goldberg, poet and publisher Ed Foster, and *Puppetmasters* author Philip Willan.

Critical acclaim for *Portraits from the Revolution*:

Most American readers will harbor a prior, casual familiarity with the Occupy Wall Street movement of 2011 based on newspaper headlines and events of the times; but for a more in-depth survey of the philosophies, approaches, and concerns of the protests, *Portraits from the Revolution: Interviews with the Protestors from Occupy Wall Street, 30 September – 8 October 2011* is the item of choice, offering unprecedented depth and detail on the history and lasting impact of the Occupy Wall Street movement.

Rob Couteau conducted a series of interviews with movement leaders; and while one might think the contents of these pieces would have been reported by the media – they were not. It's also important to note that *Portraits from the Revolution* remains the only in-depth text interview of participants that is available: so if readers wish to gain more than a casual news report's insights, *Portraits from the Revolution* is the item of choice.

Chapters explore not just each individual's actions, but their backgrounds, reasons for participating in Occupy Wall Street, and their experiences, and offers criticism of media reporting of the movement's history, intentions, and approaches. From how participants decided to react to violent antagonism against the Occupy movement to the social and political ramifications of not just Occupy but the elements it opposed, these interviews capture participants from all walks of life, from teens to full-time workers, and turns the newspaper reports into a series of personal vignettes about Occupy's deeper meaning.

Any who would better understand the events and the meaning behind news reports must turn to *Portraits from the Revolution* for a clearer vision of the "why and how" of the times.

– **Diane Donovan, *Midwest Book Review.***

Portraits from the Revolution

Interviews with the Protestors from Occupy Wall Street, 30 September – 8 October 2011

DOMINANTSTAR

ALSO BY ROB COUTEAU:

Doctor Pluss

Collected Couteau

The Sleeping Mermaid

More Collected Couteau

ROB COUTEAU

Portraits from the Revolution

Interviews with the Protestors from Occupy Wall Street, 30 September – 8 October 2011

DOMINANTSTAR

Dominantstar, New York.

First edition. Second printing. 1 2 3 4 5 6 7 8 9 10 02

Special thanks to Barney Rosset for featuring chapter two from this collection ("To Crush a Butterfly on the Wheel of a Tank") in the Evergreen Review. Other excerpts from this collec¬tion have ap-peared in a slightly altered and abridged form in Occupy the Press and Occupy Wall Street Poetry Anthology.
Cover photo by Rob Couteau.

Cover photo by Rob Couteau.

Dominantstar LLC:
dominantstarpublications.com

Author's web site:
robcouteau.com

ISBN 978-0-9966888-2-6

For Kaylee Dedrick,
and for all the victims of police abuse

Contents

Interviews with the Occupy Wall Street Protestors from 30 September 2011*

In their own words, here are a few of the dedicated men and women who have sacrificed their time and energy to provoke change in America.

While the major media continues to put words into their mouths and to spin the story every which way, this is the only lengthy text interview of actual participants that is currently available online.

Beyond any political analysis or interpretation, the most notable thing about all this is the unique atmosphere that has been created in a small park in New York. As you descend the broad marble steps into the partially sunken esplanade, you feel as if you're entering a place far away from the hectic, frenetic, anonymous atmosphere of the city. The sincerity, devotion, and generosity of these young protestors is contagious. This is the Woodstock of our time: on a much smaller scale, yet one that will certainly grow as it spreads across the country.

By incarnating the spirit of a more just and vital America, they have already accomplished something that no one can take away, distort, or destroy. This represents a new historical stepping stone, and it will serve as a focal point for all those who care enough to fight for real change.

– 4 October 2011

I arrived for my first visit to Liberty Plaza on Friday, 30 September: the fourteenth day of the occupation. Upon entering the park, I noticed two young women, Pearl and her friend Willa, seated on a mattress and politely answering questions from passersby.

Rob Couteau: Where are you from?

Pearl: Queens.

RC: And why are you here today?

Pearl: I'm here because I want to join the cause and to move toward having an actual democracy instead of an oligarchy: that the rich rule the majority of the people instead of the people ruling themselves. And that's what's happening. I'm not trying to be some sort of anarchist. I just want regular people like you and me – who actually have ideas and want to better the society – to have a shot at being on the top. Instead of, you know, you might not know much, but, if you have a lot of money, that's how you get the success you get.

RC: How old are you?

Pearl: I'm seventeen.

RC: Is this your first protest?

Pearl: Yes.

RC: There are so many university students in New York. Where are they? Why aren't they here? There should be tens of thousands of people here.

Pearl: There should be, absolutely. I don't think the country wants to admit that there's a serious problem. And other countries know what's going on; other countries are supporting us. But I think our country should really start coming together. There are other "Occupy" places. In D.C. for example …

RC: It's in over sixty cities now.

Willa: Yes. Also, we're young. We have many more years that we're going to be here. And it's going to be getting worse and worse unless we do something.

Pearl: And we don't want it to get worse. We want it to get better. When I graduate college, it's going to be one job to every twelve people, and that's because of the economy. That's because of the people that are actually ruling the country. They have no idea what they're doing.

RC: The media has criticized the fact that there's no clearly defined goal in this protest, but I think that's the beauty of it. It's a shaggy dog. And everything that you guys have done that was supposedly "wrong" has turned out right. For example, you didn't have a permit to march. The New York Civil Liberties Union offered to help you get a permit, but nobody responded. And, as a result, Officer Bologna pepper sprayed a girl named Kaylee Dedrick, along with a few other young women, and this galvanized more media attention. The fact that there's no clearly defined goal is actually creating an instant coalition. What do you think?

Pearl: Yes, certain things that happened that weren't so great actually did help to put this whole thing together. People have been coming just because they heard about the pepper-spray incident. They think it's wrong, and they want to support us. They want to be part of something.

Willa: There are a lot of things that should be protested, because there are a lot of things that are wrong right now. And it's good to be open. Somebody who doesn't care too much about the economy but really wants equal rights for everyone can come down and not feel like they don't belong here.

Pearl: Yes, because it's a big thing that everyone wants to accomplish. We're not going to keep anybody out just because they're representing something different. If you have a certain cause, you can come here and, hey, you're going to be one more person on the march. So, we're not turning anybody away.

RC: In terms of strategy, how about opening up a second site in case the police clear this site out?

Pearl: If this site gets too crowded, they're going to move it onto another block, and they're just going to do the same thing. But we're not going to leave, and we're not going to stop. We'll just move on to the next place and continue the peaceful community protest that we're trying to do. We're trying to be self-sufficient, self-sustaining, and peaceful. There are no drugs allowed here. If you're going to do drugs, you're going to have to do it somewhere else. Everyone is in a united consensus about that.

RC: What's your strategy if and when agent provocateurs show up and create violence and give the police an excuse to crack down, as happened in Seattle?

Pearl: I think every person here is on the lookout for that. If we see that someone's acting out of line, we'll ask the police to escort that person out. So, nothing major has happened. There have been a few people, but they're easily pushed out.

* * *

Next I approached Zain, a tall wiry African American man in his late thirties, who held a sign that read: "Wake Up!"

RC: I love your sign. Everyone seems to have been asleep since the days of the last great protest marches in the late Seventies.

Zain: Everybody's been asleep since the beginning of business incorporation. And turning people into numbers. That's when everybody went to sleep. Currency is pointless. We have enough resources to live on this earth peacefully and to be abundant. All we need is the earth; a couple of seeds; some water, and people. And we have that.

RC: How long have you been down here?

Zain: I came here yesterday, but I've been following it since they started, on September 17.

RC: Where are you from?

Zain: I was born in the Bronx. I came down from Middletown, New York.

RC: How long are you going to stay here?

Zain: Indefinitely.

RC: Good for you. Anything you want to add?

Zain: Just wake up, love, think about what's important, and let go of the fear.

* * *

Phil was dressed in a hooded black robe and a white rubber skull mask. He stood beneath a tree holding a scythe, garbed as the classic messenger of death.

RC: Why are you here?

Phil: Despite having a full-time job, I sympathize with what's going on. For the last ten years, the economy has been in real trouble. More and more, people are getting laid off. Jobs are being shipped overseas. Our currency is devaluating at a rapid pace: almost at a weekly pace. And jobs aren't coming back from overseas; that's for sure. Also, there are only a few people that are benefiting with the economy that we have, and the rest of us are being put in the back seat.

RC: That's why it's the ninety-nine percent, right?

Phil: Yes. Exactly.

RC: How many days have you been here?

Phil: This is my first day.

RC: You went to a lot of trouble on your first day with that costume!

Phil: I must have lost about two pounds so far, from sweating! But it's worth it. I'm glad to be here and share our experiences and to share the message. Because, really, the more we send the message, the better off we're going to be.

RC: Where are you from?

Phil: The Upper East Side.

RC: How many days are you planning to stay?

Phil: I'll be here tomorrow and next week as well, because I care. But since I have a full-time job, I'm not here as often as I'd like to be.

RC: What kind of work do you do?

Phil: I'm a concierge and a self-published author. I publish science fiction, faction, and novels.

RC: How old are you?

Phil: Forty-four.

RC: It's been a long time since this country has seen any serious kind of protest movement. Is this the start of something big?

Phil: The strange thing is, it's happening all over the world. It's happening in Spain, Greece, Israel, Egypt, and Tunisia. It's almost like a domino effect. And now, there's going to be a rally in Los Angeles, and I think there's something starting in Miami.

RC: Thanks for talking with me.

Phil: Any time!

* * *

Benny was dressed in one of the most elaborate costumes in the park, featuring a gas mask and a black robe bearing the message: "Work, Consume, Be Silent, Die. I Rely on Your Apathy." A visitor from Australia, he's a dedicated antinuke activist and is committed to shutting down Indian Point nuclear power plant in upstate New York.

RC: Why are you here?

Benny: For a number of reasons. There's a rally tomorrow, a no-nukes rally, which is really crucial, because we just had a nuclear meltdown in Fukushima, Japan. And Indian Point, upstate, is leaking, and it's ticking away. In a few years time, we want it decommissioned. Otherwise, it's probably going to be operating for another thirty years, and the risk is high. We could have a Fukushima here at any time, in New York City.

We've got to change our ways. This whole occupation is to wake people up. They've got to act. Each one of us is very important. We've got to take that information and change their attitude toward the whole. We've got to be holistic about the effect we have on the planet, and for future generations, because it's at a crisis point now. It's time to get out there.

RC: From the very start of this movement, I've had an intuition that it's absolutely now or never. This rally has to take off, or else the country is never going to wake up.

Benny: It's a wake-up call, absolutely. It's also a "screaming out" by scientists; environmental people all over the world have been saying it for ages. And now, young people. And through all this, we can move toward sustainable energy.

Hopefully, all these financiers out here will start directing their energies – their financial energies – to help transform the planet and heal the planet and all the beings that live on it. At the moment, it's dying, because of the culture that's developed up till now: the consumerist culture. Now we've got to think in terms of how we get back to the earth.

RC: So you're really saying that our energy has to be channeled to this theme.

Benny: Yes.

RC: How old are you, and how long are you going to remain here?

Benny: I turn sixty-six tomorrow. If the energy's good, I'm going to stay here for a while.

* * *

Zuni was hard not to notice since she seemed to be everywhere at once, interacting with the various groups that composed the core of the movement. She was also walking around topless, surrounded by passersby bearing startled expressions.

RC: How old are you?

Zuni: I'm thirty-seven.

RC: Why are you here?

Zuni: For a lot of reasons. I don't even know where to start; there are so many issues. But my basic reason for being here is for equality. Not just for this country but for everyone in the world. There are enough resources to go around. It doesn't have to be like this, with people starving on the side of the street or cold every night.

RC: Where are you from?

Zuni: New Jersey.

RC: How long are you going to stay?

Zuni: For as long as it takes.

RC: Have you been harassed by the police for walking around topless?

Zuni: No.

RC: How long have you been doing that?

Zuni: Since day one. Fourteen days.

RC: Why are you doing it? Is there a reason?

Zuni: To exercise my rights before I lose them. We live in a police state, so we have to exercise all our rights or they slowly take them away. Sweep it under a rug; next thing, it's gone.

RC: Anything you'd like to add?

Zuni: If people want to come down and join us, that would be awesome. We need all the people we can get if we're really going to take Wall Street down.

RC: Why do you think there are so few people here, considering the fact that we're surrounded by major universities in New York? If this were 1968, all those universities would be emptied out.

Zuni: Because education today is actually indoctrination. A lot of these people are indoctrinated. And they're just comfortable enough not to get up off their asses and do something about it.

RC: Is it selfishness? Are they more concerned about getting the "A-plus"?

Zuni: Yes, I think so. But capitalism doesn't work. We've seen that.

RC: Is there a lack of empathy in this generation?

Zuni: There is a lack of empathy, yes. And this generation, these kids didn't "go outside and play." When we were kids, we went outside and played. These kids sat in front of a TV, or video game, or whatever. So, they're kind of in their own world anyway.

RC: They're victims of an electronic hallucination produced by corporations.

Zuni: Yes.

* * *

One of the most articulate and devoted activists that I had the pleasure of meeting that day, Yvonne wore a blond Marie-Antoinette wig and a blouse fashioned from an American flag. The stars on the flag were covered with three horizontally placed dollar bills. She also donned red satin shorts and black fishnet stockings.

RC: I love your outfit.

Yvonne: Thank you!

RC: Where are you from?

Yvonne: Washington Heights.

RC: How many days have you been here?

Yvonne: On and off, since the first night. I slept out here the very first night, and I've been coming back every day that I can. Every morning, every afternoon, every evening that I can actually make time to come here. I really wish I could be here full-time.

RC: What else do you do?

Yvonne: I'm an actress and a playwright. But currently, as a job, I work for a wind farm. I promote wind energy: switching New Yorkers over from coal and nuclear to wind. That's part of my activism as well. So, I'm pretty much a full-time activist.

RC: Where are you from?

Yvonne: I was born in Smithtown, Long Island, but I grew up in Tampa, Florida.

RC: How old are you?

Yvonne: I'm twenty-eight.

RC: What's the main reason that you're here?

Yvonne: I'm here for a lot of different reasons, much like everyone else. But to be specific, corporations control our government; they control our politics. The government does not protect the people. As a matter-of-fact, it has become the exact opposite. What I mean by that is, just to offer a very specific example: the BP oil spill poisoned the Gulf of Mexico about a year and a half ago. Hundreds of thousands of people have been poisoned by that spill. A lot of people have died. A lot of people have been terminally ill ever since. Children have died. I mean, it's utterly insane.

But the media is not talking about it, and the media will not talk about it. If any reporter were to come out and break the story on national news, it would be utter chaos, because over six million people swam in the Gulf since that oil spill. Six million people came into contact. And that's from looking at the tourists' stats and the Census Bureau. So, just to give a very specific example, BP poisoned the Gulf of Mexico. They made a lot of money off that accident. The people of the Gulf have been injured; they're poisoned. And our government is protecting BP because they are controlled by BP, partly, and by big oil, and by big coal. It's just insane. It's gotten out of control.

RC: It's one of the most disgusting unreported stories.

Yvonne: Yes. That, and all the insider trading that went on prior to 9/11. I know people don't want to talk about it; it's a very hard topic to discuss. There was a lot of insider trading leading up to 9/11. And the 9/11 first responders were also exposed to toxic chemicals, and they're dying, and they're not getting their medical expenses paid for.

I do not want my money to go toward war. I want my money to go to people who stood up and went to clean up the Gulf of Mexico or to clean up the World Trade Center. That's where I want my money to go, not to the war.

RC: A lot of the Establishment Left have said that the protestors need to pick a specific issue. But I feel that what they're doing is much smarter than that. By having no specific issue, it's created an instant coalition.

Yvonne: Yes. No command; no one goal. I like to say that there are no rules in the revolution. In any revolution that has ever happened, there were people who were fighting for a lot of different reasons. There are no rules in the revolution.

RC: So you feel that it's attracting many more people than it would if there were just one specific goal.

Yvonne: Yes. People come here for different reasons. I'm here to revoke the rights of corporations: to get corporate money out of politics. To revoke their rights and to hold corporations accountable for their crimes against humanity. There are people here that are only pissed off about the fact that we're at war. There are people that are only pissed off about the fact that Troy Davis was murdered. There are people that are only pissed off about the fact that they're unemployed or have student debt. But, in the end, it all goes back to corporate greed, and corporations controlling our government, and there being no real regulation. Our politicians are not protecting us. They are doing the exact opposite. They are only protecting the corporations.

RC: Can you say a few words about the outfit you're

wearing?

Yvonne: As I said, I'm an actress and a street performer. I'm wearing an American flag, and the flag is backward. Dollar bills are covering up the stars, because Americans are consumers, and corporations look at America as a dollar sign. Every child that is born is going to be "X"-amount of dollars for each individual corporation. We're just a symbol of money; we're consumers. So, I have three one-dollar bills upside down. And the flag is backward and upside down, because America is backward and upside down.

I'm wearing a Marie-Antoinette wig because the wig symbolizes the French Revolution, which was also a class war. And I have a little flag that says "End War Now," because, again, I don't want my tax dollars going toward war. I want my tax dollars going toward things that really matter. And I wish everyone here would join the "End War Now" cause, since a lot of our problems are rooted to the fact that we spend over a trillion of our tax dollars on war.

* * *

While poking through donations in the Occupy Wall Street Library – an eclectic assortment of literature stacked in cardboard boxes, including work by Aeschylus, Aristotle, Shakespeare, and Henry James – Melissa handed me a book titled An Atlas of Radical Cartography, *saying, "I was going to read it, but maybe you'd like to read it first." Then I noticed her sign, which read: "Renewable Resources Recharge Earth."*

RC: How old are you?

Melissa: I'm twenty-one.

RC: Where are you from?

Melissa: I came from Virginia.

RC: Why are you here today?

Melissa: There are a multitude of reasons. I'm here because renewable resources are hard to get. Or health care. I mean, look all over the world. There are so many countries that have access to health care. Here, it costs so much just to fix a minor fracture. And that's really disappointing, when we have all the doctors available.

RC: This could be the spark not only for a nationwide protest but also for a 1960s-like movement. Do you think this will happen?

Melissa: Hopefully. Well, it's already started to happen. If you look at the map over there, there's a bunch of protests all over the country. The numbers are growing, and people are starting to realize, and to open their eyes, and to shy away from these biased views that are shown through media, such as CNN or Fox News.

RC: Where are you staying?

Melissa: Here, this is my home!

RC: How many nights have you slept in the park?

Melissa: Two out of the last three.

RC: What's it been like?

Melissa: Difficult to sleep. If you've ever heard of Chinese torture methods, they use a water-drip method to torture their victims, by dripping water on the forehead incessantly. Feeling rain all over your body is keeping your body in alert all night, and so finding sleep is difficult.

RC: Do you have a sleeping bag?

Melissa: Yes.

RC: Did you arrive here alone or with a friend?

Melissa: I came with a friend, but he returned to D.C.

so that he could start a protest back home. But this is really where the action is; he's missing out! [Laughs]

RC: Where is your family from?

Melissa: Vietnam. My grandfather was an ambassador from Indochina stationed in Burma. Luckily, we were able to get out of the country before the war.

* * *

A petite African American woman in her late twenties, Lamar was walking through the park accompanied by some friends and carrying a sign that read: "Hug Me."

RC: What's the "Hug Me" thing about?

Lamar: I found this sign, and I thought it was very appropriate. It's a good message. Some people need to be hugged; do you know what I mean?

RC: It *is* a good message. Empathy!

Lamar: Right. It's also all about solidarity: human solidarity. I feel this sign embodies that. So, I just went ahead with it.

RC: What's the main reason that you're here today, besides hugging people?

Lamar: I think most of us are here because of the economic situation in the country and in the world. As you know, a lot of people on Wall Street, we bailed them out. And they're not being held accountable for all the money that they got.

RC: We bailed them out, and now we're being told we have to "cut back" even though this country is awash with money. The top one percent has more money than ever.

Lamar: Exactly. That's my main reason. The whole money system is horrible. The way money is created is horrible. And the system is made so that there are always poor people. I suppose that's OK as long as people have what they need, but that is not the case. And when that happens, then this happens.

RC: How old are you?

Lamar: I'm twenty-eight.

RC: Where are you from?

Lamar: I'm originally from Panama.

RC: Where do you live now?

Lamar: In Brooklyn, in Bed-Stuy.

RC: How old were you when you arrived from Panama?

Lamar: I was seventeen. It was just a couple of days before I turned eighteen.

RC: Many of the established left-wing groups in New York are criticizing this protest. They're saying that you should pick one thing to focus on. But I think it's brilliant that there isn't one thing, because now you have an automatic coalition, which is of interest to everyone. This is the ninety-nine percent that is getting screwed over in the country. Do you agree?

Lamar: I do. For example, the first time I came, on the day of the Troy Davis march, it was a little confusing, because there was a Troy Davis March and there was also the Ninety-nine Percent March. But then the two things joined. It got limited coverage; not a lot of people knew about it. But I think it was beautiful, how people were helping each other's issues. This is also part of what's going on here. A lot of it is about solidarity.

I think it's a legitimate criticism that they're making; I understand where they're coming from. It's not like I don't see their point. For it to have a faster effect, it probably needs to be focused; that's true. But there's a lot of beauty in the fact that it's including many issues that are somehow interrelated. They are the issues of the ninety-nine percent, and I suppose that's the main thing. That is the common denominator.

RC: If you had to pick one issue, it really is the ninety-nine percent: that we're all part of the ninety-nine percent.

Lamar: Right. The issue is that there's a ninety-nine percent as opposed to a one-hundred percent, you know?

RC: Great point; that's the main thing. So, if you're part of the ninety-nine percent, whether you're the part that cares about Troy Davis or the part that cares about paying too many taxes, it's not important. If you're part of the ninety-nine percent, that's the issue, right?

Lamar: Yes.

RC: Have you slept in the park?

Lamar: No. I'm going to do that tomorrow, because tomorrow there's a march at 3:00 p.m. and I'm going to want to stay.

RC: How many days have you been here?

Lamar: This is my second time.

RC: Was the first time before the pepper-spray incident?

Lamar: Before, because the pepper-spray incident was on Saturday.

RC: Did the NYPD attitude change at all since that incident? Have they pulled back a bit?

Lamar: Absolutely. When I came that day, there was almost one cop per person. I was like: Do they really have nothing better to do than stand here? I remember thinking, "There must be so much crime. This is the prefect moment to commit a crime; all the cops are here!" Literally, we were surrounded by cops.

RC: Lining the park.

Lamar: Yes.

RC: Were any of them in the park?

Lamar: After 11 p.m. when people were not allowed to make any noise, there were some kids with drums that were superlow, like no noise, and they came over and said, "You can't drum." They were watching, just trying to intimidate.

RC: So, it changed after that.

Lamar: Yes.

RC: Do you think it changed because, after the pepper-spray assault, some of the media arrived and the police were afraid of any coverage of a second incident?

Lamar: Yes, that shifted it a lot. This movement had almost no coverage, and the media attention it did get was like, "Oh, somebody got arrested; there are these kids on Wall Street, blah, blah, blah." No real coverage.

I think that's the way that Mayor Bloomberg was attacking this movement. But after that – with the media, and with independent videos on YouTube – obviously everyone knows what they're doing, you know? They were literally intimidating everybody. I mean, nobody is being hurt; there's really nothing actually happening. There was no need for all those cops to be here. I mean, if you want a couple of cars here and there, OK, fine. But we were surrounded.

RC: It's because you guys are threatening the status quo. You have the potential to totally threaten the status quo.

Lamar: That's true.

RC: I'm not saying this justifies it, but they are afraid, much more than you may realize.

Lamar: I suppose. But it's not a violent movement, and, because of that, nobody has, whatever, a machete, or anything to hurt somebody else.

RC: This is also why the Establishment brings in agent provocateurs to create violence, as they did in Seattle. What do you think is going to happen if they use agent provocateurs? One girl said, "We'll recognize them; we'll take them aside and bring them to the police."

Lamar: If it happens, I hope that people are able to recognize them. That's really what worries me. I wasn't here for it, but, the first time I came, somebody told me that there was an undercover cop trying to figure out what was next, and what they were doing, and "What's that whole assembly about?" But people recognized him and said, "You have to go!" And I'm so happy for that.

RC: Sometimes, they're so obvious! [Laughs]

Lamar: I truly hope that they *are* obvious.

RC: I'm fifty-five years old; I grew up in the Sixties. Every night at the dinner table we had the television on, and we could see the names of the boys who were killed in Vietnam, the body count. The body bags were coming back to the middle class. And that was what changed things: the working class and the middle class, the majority of the country, was directly affected. That's why I have hope for this movement, because it also involves the middle class.

Lamar: Yes, it affects the middle class, but the problem is that a lot of the middle class don't know it's happening. A lot of people still don't know about this. A lot of people in Brooklyn don't know.

RC: So we need to wake people up.

Lamar: Yes.

RC: OK, I'm ready for my hug.

Lamar: [Laughs] Thank you!

* * *

I was about to exit the park when I met Lauren, who was seated under some trees beside a half dozen small paintings displayed on the ground. I was drawn by the fine quality of her work, and we began to talk about why she was here.

RC: Where are you from?

Lauren: Baltimore, Maryland, but I live in Brooklyn. It's one of the only places that you can still find affordable housing.

RC: [Pointing to a row of six acrylic portraits, each measuring about eight-by-twelve inches.] These are very well done. How long have you been a painter?

Lauren: For about twelve or thirteen years. I started when I was in high school.

RC: Do you work in the city?

Lauren: Yes, for a small publishing house in Manhattan. I do graphic design, layouts, and stuff like that.

RC: How old are you?

Lauren: I'm twenty-seven.

RC: What's the main reason that you're here today?

Lauren: I came on Sunday, just to check it out, to see what was going on. I heard a lot about it, and I had a friend who was involved in it. So I came by, and I was really inspired by the people who came down. I saw other artists painting on the street and making signs. It was a collective of people just peacefully gathering, and I related to that and wanted to document the people here. I think that's what they're hoping for: to be seen as just ordinary people.

RC: That's a unique idea because, nowadays, everyone's so obsessed with technological documentation.

Lauren: Right, making a video.

RC: But you're doing it with just paint and a brush. Do you use an easel, or do you work sitting down?

Lauren: Today I've just been sitting on the lawn.

RC: Are these on canvas?

Lauren: No, they're on cardboard. I got the idea of doing it on cardboard because all the protest signs are on cardboard.

RC: How long do people pose for you?

Lauren: Anywhere from thirty to forty minutes. I try not to keep them here all day long.

RC: They don't get jittery? This is a very jittery generation!

Lauren: I try to talk to them and ask where they're from and why are they're here: stuff like that. Sometimes, they're with a friend, and so they talk with their friend and aren't totally bored out of their minds. [Laughs]

RC: What do you plan to do with the paintings after you're finished?

Lauren: Tonight, I'm going to start to lace them together, or sew them together, or connect them in some way. And then put them on display. And hopefully, by the next day, do some more portraits. Then I'll connect those onto the ones from the day before.

RC: So you're making a sort of collage.

Lauren: Yes, a collage of people who have been sort of amalgamated since I've been sitting here, painting.

RC: Is there anything you'd like to add about being here and the whole experience?

Lauren: It's really interesting. It's definitely growing. And I'm happy to see this happening. For myself, I didn't come down here just to make paintings and portraits and stuff like that. It wasn't about that. A lot of people are frustrated with the financial system and how things have been going, myself included. And so, it's interesting to see a bunch of people coming together, trying to see something change. And I hope it does.

RC: There are so many people living in New York. If this were 1968, there would be tens of thousands of students here. But so far the students are mostly staying at home. I think it's really shameful. What do you think?

Lauren: Some of it's been poorly covered. I don't think people really know what it is. It may be miscovered, and they're like, "Oh, it's just a bunch of ratty kids that are getting their asses kicked by the police." But I think that anyone who's come down here has had a completely different experience. Whether you're skeptical of it or not, it isn't quite what it's been portrayed as. But I think it's growing. It's only been two weeks. So, who knows?

RC: Next week, the Transit Workers Union, which has 38,000 members in New York City, is going to be rallying here. In America in the Sixties, there was little connection between the unions and the students. But in Paris, they almost shut down the government; the unions united with the students. And now this is happening at the *beginning* of the movement. Talk about being ignored by the media; this is a remarkable story!

Lauren: Right! And the airline pilots were here yesterday. It's another case of people who really could be making more money. You know, they do so much for so many people; why aren't they being taken care of for the work that they do?

RC: I have a friend who's a stewardess who told me that pilots are notorious for voting Republican. So, for pilots to come down here is really extraordinary.

Lauren: Right. Maybe that's why it isn't covered. I think a lot of people are frustrated. I mean, it really is ninety-nine percent of the people! And maybe they're skeptical and not exactly sure. But I think, deep down, they're probably a little frustrated. Why wouldn't they be? What happened in 2008 with the Wall Street bailouts is unfathomable. So, that's something that ninety-nine percent of the people have in common.

Obviously I don't know what's going to happen. But I came down to do what I can.

RC: Thanks so much for talking.

Lauren: No problem. It was awesome to meet you!

---

* Published on 4 October 2011 at tygersofwrath.com.

To Crush a Butterfly on the Wheel of a Tank. Marching with the Occupy Demonstrators on 5 October 2011*

Anyone who grew up in the 1960s will recall the singular image of construction workers – or "hard hats," as they were called – mercilessly beating the antiwar demonstrators who marched through Lower Manhattan. As I pointed out to many of the young people I interviewed on September 30 at Liberty Plaza, the fact that organizations such as the Transit Workers Union (TWU) were now pledging to join the protestors was nothing less than extraordinary when viewed in this historical context. I added that, in the Paris revolts of 1968, the solidarity of the unions and students had nearly brought down the government, but nothing comparable had ever happened here, in the days of rage, during the Sixties and early Seventies.

Those conversations occurred on the fourteenth day of the occupation. In the days that followed, other miracles appeared, one more astonishing than the next. First, the United Steelworkers Union pledged its support. Then a group of Marine veterans joined the protestors to "protect them from the police" – even donning full dress uniforms as they "stood guard."

So when the transit workers decided to rally, I knew I had to be there to witness what would certainly become an emblematic image of our time.

The TWU and several other unions were planning on assembling at the Federal Building at Foley Square, then leading an enormous rally back to the park. Because of a rare eye illness that causes an extreme thinning of the corneas (Keratoconus), I couldn't afford to get pepper sprayed. To risk it was to risk permanent blindness.

Therefore, I initially planned to stay in Zuccotti Park (the official name of Liberty Plaza) and to await the marchers there.

I arrived at 3:00 p.m. from upstate New York. There were about 2,000 people on the first day that I'd visited, on September 30, but now the crowd had grown much larger. There was also a broader social spectrum of protestors: those of all ages, including the first sprinkling of union workers bearing picket signs.

About an hour later, a core member of the Occupy group announced there would be a "permitless" rally leaving momentarily for Foley Square, where they would join the unions that were assembling en masse. Afterward, everyone would march back to Liberty Plaza. Despite my trepidation about sustaining serious injury, I was swept up in the exhilaration of the moment and I knew that I had to join them.

I trailed behind a small group of protestors who were holding a large America flag with a message scrawled on the front. When one of the young men's arms grew tired, I offered to take his place as we continued along the avenue with a crowd of several thousand. I figured: either I'll be safe here, behind this flag, or I'll get attacked for desecrating it. Indeed, as the police eyeballed us, we were careful not to let it touch the ground. A brightly tattooed young woman who was holding the flag beside me also held a sign with her other hand, but as we marched I could only read the back of it: the top of a pizza box.

Although my life is dedicated to writing, it wasn't the words that were important now: it was the direct, visceral experience of simply being there. However, I later discovered that she was a recent graduate of accounting and had been searching for work for many months, all to no avail, and that's what the sign addressed. I told her that when I'd graduated with an arts degree in 1978, I never expected to find a serious job; but, back then, for an accountant to have had so much trouble seeking "gainful employment" would have been unthinkable.

Some of the police who lined the street along the way seemed fairly relaxed about everything. One African American officer was even smiling and nodding his head, keeping time to our chants as if he approved. A few cops just seemed bored or indifferent. But others resembled Nazi storm troopers just waiting for someone to mess up. Those were the ones with a sort of screwed up, intense expression on their faces: as if their skin were about to explode. Mostly, these were the ones with gold badges or wearing white shirts: the supervisors.

Once we entered Foley Square we were engulfed in a much larger crowd. The unions were there in force, making speeches and carrying colorful and often witty signs.

After mingling with the protestors, I decided to take the train back and to wait with camera in hand at Liberty Plaza for the arrival of the union members. But before I could do so, I had to ask the police for permission to enter a subway station. This was a foreboding of the bad things to come later on. Fortunately, these rank-and-file blue shirts, mostly African Americans, remained professional and polite.

By sunset there were about 20,000 people marching around the plaza. As it grew dark, the lighting equipment from various media outlets cast sections of the street under an eerie, bone-white glow. The chanting continued without interruption while the demonstrators grew more and more energized. Although the marchers had taken over Liberty Street, the police had erected metal barricades along Broadway and were keeping the protestors on the sidewalk so that traffic could flow unimpeded. But I wondered how much longer this ever-swelling crowd could be contained.

I'd only had about two hours of sleep the previous night, so after absorbing these impressive events and watching the marchers rally in increasing numbers – some of them splitting off to march on Wall Street without a permit – I decided to leave at 7:30 p.m. and I headed for the train.

It took quite a while to walk those few blocks. We were tightly packed behind the barricades on the sidewalk, and most of the crowd remained stationary, chanting to the police to "join us." Some shouted slogans about how police pensions were threatened as well: that they, too, were part of the ninety-nine percent. But these were friendly chants, not violent or confrontational ones, and the atmosphere continued to remain positive, at least as far as the behavior of the protestors was concerned.

I finally approached a subway, where I encountered several cops stationed beside the entrance, but they minded their own business as I continued down the steps.

As I later learned, about thirty minutes after I'd left, certain police officers became violent. There's a new video circulating that's far worse than the pepper-spray incident. It captures a white-shirted supervisor viciously beating the protestors: smashing his club into a crowd with great force, swinging it back and forth – over and over, like a madman. Or rather, not *like* a madman but as only a madman would. Apparently, the supervisors decided to block the entrances to certain subways stations, and the crowd, which was immense by this time, had nowhere else to go, so it spilled into the street. And then, the "white shirts" went berserk.

It reminded me of how, during the Algerian War, the Paris police had closed certain métro stations and then herded the fleeing demonstrators down the steps – where they encountered locked gates, were beaten to death, and later dumped into the Seine. The most infamous murder was that of a young pregnant woman.

It seems as if the tactics never change; each generation simply has to relearn them, often from scratch. Mussolini had his "black shirts" while here, in America, we have our "white shirts."

Perhaps one could say: "Thank God for the abject stupidity of some of these supervisors, because they're doing more and more each day to galvanize the protestors: to bring them out in larger numbers and to turn the nation against the police." But these vicious cops are merely the embodiment of a visceral hatred that the ruling class increasingly harbors for the commoners: the "consumers."

It's the same fight that's been going on throughout the centuries. And it will never end until something more fundamental changes, once and for all. But this time, it's being videotaped and broadcast by ordinary people instead of being suppressed or selectively edited by the powers that be.

Perhaps holding a digital camera aloft and passively recording such crimes will prove to be a form of Gandhian nonviolence that engenders a broader support from the masses. Perhaps passivity can be transformed into "passive resistance." But those cameras will be held in place only for so long before someone starts to throw one. These particular cops are playing with fire and, so far, no one in the government seems to understand this. As one of the older gentlemen at Foley Square said to me earlier that afternoon, "Where are the Bobby Kennedys of our time? I'm a lifelong Democratic, but no one in the Democratic Party seems to care about us anymore."

"Yes," I replied. "And because of that, the people have taken to the street. Now, it's up to us."

* This photo essay was originally published in the *Evergreen Review* in February 2012.

Benny Zable, a sixty-year-old antinuke activist from Australia. When asked why he had joined the movement, he said: “We’ve got to be holistic about the effect we have on the planet, because it’s a crisis point now. It’s time to get out there.”

Signs created by the young artists at Liberty Plaza, many of whom were university students burdened with enormous student-loan debt. The messages drew the attention of many pedestrians who had been previously unaware of the movement.

A finance worker who said it all without saying a word, with a dollar bill taped over his mouth and a sign constructed from a pizza box.

"We live in a police state, so we have to exercise our rights or they slowly take them away. My basic reason for being here is for equality. Not just for this country but for everyone in the world. There are enough resources to go around. It doesn't have to be like this, with people starving on the side of the street or cold every night."

”

Demonstrators amassing in Zuccotti Park near Liberty and Broadway, standing beside the Occupy Wall Street Library (along the wall on left; later destroyed by the police).

“Children of the revolution,” seated beside university students who said “We’re young. We have many more years that we’re going to be here. And it’s going to be getting worse and worse unless we do something.”

Stationed at key points along the park, organizers addressed the crowd via the People's Mic: a "human microphone" that bypassed New York City's regulations against amplified electronic sound.

Police following us, batons at the ready, as we marched along Broadway and approached the Federal Building.

"Power to the Peaceful." One of the thousands of protestors that occupied Foley Square on 5 October 2011.

A Pratt University Art Student, a Volunteer Librarian, a "Grandmother for Peace," a Teamster and an Ironworker. What Do They All Have in Common?

5 October: At the southern edge of the park, David sat with his friends Jess and Hannah on the floor, painting cardboard signs. The three eighteen-year-old art students spoke about the exorbitant costs of Pratt University, the burden of student loans, and the various reasons they'd joined the protest. A continual roar of 20,000 marchers encircling Liberty Plaza added a booming accompaniment to my animated conversation with David, who spoke about his experience at Occupy Wall Street.

Rob Couteau: Is this your first day?

David: No, I've spent the night here, two or three times.

RC: You slept here all night?

David: Yes. I didn't plan on sleeping here; one day, I just showed up. I was talking with so many people that, soon, it was about 5:00 in the morning, and there was a march. And I was like, "Oh, all right. We'll just stay till 9:00 a.m." That was the first night I was here; it was amazing. Then, a few other nights, I biked home and grabbed a sleeping bag. Actually, it was just a blanket. I was lucky; I didn't get any rain.

RC: So you had a place to stay in Brooklyn, but you expressed solidarity and stayed and slept in the park. What's the toughest thing about sleeping here?

David: The hard ground. Otherwise, it's actually very nice. There's food, and everyone's very friendly, including the police officers ninety-percent of the time. And even when they're not friendly, they're usually just passive-aggressive. You're sleeping on the street, but you feel safe. I can leave my stuff out, and I don't have to worry about people taking it. This was before September 30: before there were so many people. I don't know if the attitude has changed, but I doubt it.

RC: Why are you here?

David: I have homework; I should be at home! But my friends wanted to come, and now I've been here for a few weeks. When I first arrived, it was one of the more inspiring moments that I've experienced in a long time. I've done activism before, but it's always been people angry, and marching, and just saying things. This was the first time that I could see *action.* I could feel the solidarity, power, and devotion behind the movement. I went home, and that's all I could think about. I was excited to come back, and I've been returning ever since.

This is a movement that's really important. You hear people in the media talking about all the problems we have, like, "Oh, it's a hard problem to solve this" or "It's a hard problem to solve that." The truth is, they may be hard to solve, but they're not hard problems to think of solutions for. It's very clear. There's an excess of wealth in the hands of a minority. If we redistributed that wealth, then so any of our problems – from abortion issues to sexual assault, poverty, food issues, war and violence – could be solved by redistributing wealth in America. And many of those problems stem from our economic troubles. So, I'm glad that there are people out here, taking action.

RC: Where are you from?

David: I'm from Boston, Hannah's from San Francisco and Jess is from Long Island.

RC: I feel that this is the Woodstock of our time, metaphorically speaking.

David: Yes! That's what's really exciting. This is the biggest progressive movement that people have seen since the Sixties. It's really wonderful. My generation especially is so pacified, and all about sitting on their asses, and turning on the TV. We expect things to be given to us. So, it's really nice to see people with privilege getting out into the street.

RC: Are you and your friends an exception to your generation? The fact that you're offering your time and energy to come here and lend your support – are you an exception, or are you in the avant-garde of your generation?

David: I don't know if we're an exception. I don't think I'd separate myself from my generation. But we're lucky to have broken out of this.

RC: Is your generation is more narcissistic than the ones that have preceded it?

David: No; I think that we hate ourselves more.

RC: But that's part of the clinical definition of narcissism!

David: Yes. Well, I don't know. But I don't think my generation is so by nature, because we grew up and we remember what it was like to not have the Internet. That's something that's frightening. It's scary, because we're the last generation that's ever going to know that. I think we communicate differently than other generations; so we have some issues concerning communicating and taking action.

RC: So, you're raising the issue of *apathy* rather than a lack of *empathy*, right?

David: Exactly. It's not that anyone in my generation is deprived or lacking anything; I think we're just pacified. And I don't know if that's our fault. To a certain degree, I think we need to accept it.

In sophomore year in high school, I went through a conscious effort to kill my TV. I wouldn't watch television no matter what. If I was in a room full of people and the TV was turned on, I'd leave. I'm not as intense about that as I used to be. But I think it's really important to take on only the messages that you choose. And TV is pretty destructive. Our generation is given a lot more to entertain them, and given more in the vein of false consciousness. So it's significantly harder for us, more than any other generation, to liberate ourselves and to see the real issues in the world.

In Hinduism, that's like the veil of *maya*. It's harder for us to take away the veil of *maya*, because there are a greater amount of things that distract us.

RC: Yes. But a more comprehensive translation of the Sanskrit term *maya* includes the notion of *building blocks*: the building blocks of matter, from which all illusion is formed. Your generation is the first to use these particular building blocks to organize a nationwide protest: keeping others abreast of events by text messaging from a paddy wagon, or by organizing protest rallies from the Internet. You use the electronic hallucination produced by corporations to fight against those very corporations and to overturn the corrupt power structure. Another example is the pepper-spray incident, which was videotaped from every conceivable angle so that the police could no longer say, "You edited the video."

David: Yes. That's one thing about our generation: we don't necessarily get up and go out a lot, but, when we do, we do it right! [Laughs] That's one thing I've been amazed at; the political ideas here are really dead-on. One of the issues with the old Left is that it was black-and-white. It was like: "Oh, I'm a *Marxist*" or "I'm a *social-*

ist." I think the people here are much less about separating things into categories. They see how everything connects, and they see how all social issues are attached to other social issues, which is really important. Many look at things holistically, which is something that most politics is lacking. So, it's exciting. It's disappointing that movements like this don't happen more often. But, at the same time, it's superinspiring when they do. When they do happen, they're really thought out. People are really considerate and make things better using the tools that we have.

RC: What will this lead to, in the end?

David: The change that will come is a cultural change. That's why I'm studying art, because art is what determines culture. We need to shift the culture of apathy, which is brought about by technology, and change it to something that's a culture of activism. Which technology can be a tremendous tool for, but, right now, it's being subverted, and it's being used as a tool of pacification.

RC: It's not only your generation that's being tempted into this technological addiction via Internet and other forms of high tech. Even someone my age has to literally pull himself away from this technology. You know, in French, the word for entertainment is *divertissement*, to be diverted.

David: Yes, exactly!

RC: But for an artist, that's not a true entertainment. An artist doesn't want to be diverted; he wants to be profoundly *moved* by an artistic product. Instead of creating objects of diversion, he's trying to create heavenly objects. So, artists especially have to be very careful about pulling themselves away from this technology.

David: Yes. And that's one thing that upsets me about

being at Pratt: how many students watch TV and spend their time on blogs and stuff online. That's what's crazy about the Internet. It's really a razor's edge. On the one hand, it's a tremendous tool of the people, right? Like free information, free participation: the masses versus everyone else. It could be this amazing equalizer. Or it could be this amazing tool for those in power: to oppress.

RC: Anything you'd like to add?

David: I'm glad that you're out here. It was great to talk with you!

* * *

8 October: Stephen Boyer is a twenty-seven-year-old volunteer librarian at Liberty Plaza. He's also editor of the Occupy Wall Street Poetry Anthology, *which published its first issue three days after this interview.*

RC: Where are you from?

Stephen Boyer: I grew up in Southern California, went to art school in San Francisco, and have lived all over the world. I've been in New York a year and a half.

RC: How long have you lived overseas?

SB: About two and a half years. I just spent the summer in London. I returned about two weeks ago.

RC: How did you first hear about this?

SB: My friend was one of the main guys at the info booth. I hadn't heard about it, and, the night I got back, he was just going crazy with info about what was happening. So I came the next night.

RC: What day was that?

SB: September 28. It was a rainy day, and I wasn't expecting much when I got here. But ten hours later, I was like: "All right!" [Laughs] And I've been coming ever since. I'm helping out at the library, and I'm doing a poetry assembly every Friday night, on these steps. Last week we had two and a half hours of open-mic poetry. This week, the library is giving us money to compile everyone's poetry. We're going to print it each week, and I'm really excited about that.

RC: What did you study at school?

SB: Creative writing and sociology.

RC: That's sort of perfect for what you're doing right now, isn't it?

SB: [Laughs] Yes.

RC: What made you decide to work at the People's Library?

SB: I was originally part of the arts-and-culture group. Last Friday, when I was setting up the poetry assembly, I was hanging out with the librarians and talking with them about putting together a zine for the poetry people. And they loved it and wanted to give me money to print it. Then I just fell in love with the library. It's nice to have a person from the arts-and-culture group working on the poetry assembly. It's a good fit for me, because it works with both groups. So I'm here.

RC: The last interview I did was with three eighteen-year-old Pratt University art students, on October 5. That was the day of the Foley Square rally. While we were speaking, I realized that there's a big focus here on people who are interested in the arts. Would you agree?

SB: Yes.

RC: In that sense, do you think this is a bit different from the rallies of the Sixties and Seventies?

SB: Yes. A lot of people my age have gone to school to become artists. Nowadays, if you don't have an MFA, it's really hard to be an artist and to be paid. But we're all crushed with student-loan debt; it's impossible to live. So, as an artist, what's happening here is directly connected with what we're struggling with on a day-to-day basis.

RC: On October 5, I marched for the first time since 1979. The girl who was marching beside me was carrying a sign that said she was an accountant who hadn't found a job in over a year. When I graduated in the late Seventies, most of my friends and I had art degrees, which meant that we never really expected to find a real job. But now, even a person with a degree in accountancy doesn't expect to get a job. Doesn't that say a lot?

SB: Yes. None of my friends who have gone to school has a serious job. Everyone's working in a restaurant or doing something sketchy to make rent. I didn't expect to come out of school and to become a billionaire, but I expected to have some sort of security, and I don't.

RC: What's the most special thing about being here?

SB: I've been here for a few days now, and I started sleeping here, which I didn't expect to do. If you do come down, it sort of sweeps you away: the amount of diversity and the different things happening. There seems to be something for everyone. Whether you're an artist or into politics, finances, food – or whatever your interests are – there's a place for you here. It's like a new city inside one of the greatest cities in the world. This is where everyone that's cool in New York is, you know?

RC: What do you think this is going to lead to? Where will we be a year from now?

SB: Hopefully, we'll get an amendment to the constitution. There's enough of an energy swirl so that we're not just going to go down without something changing for us. Now we can see that we're all equally angry and equally determined to change the course of what's going on in this country. I don't think it will stop until things change for the better.

There's more than one issue that we're fighting for. If we just picked one or two demands, we'd be pigeonholed as the people who wanted just a couple of things. In fact, we want a lot more than one or two things. There are thousands of different demands, and I think they're all worthwhile and should all be looked at.

RC: Recently, there's been an attempt to articulate a platform of issues that the group wants to focus on. I saw something about this on their Web site.

SB: Yes. I know that people are talking about creating a list of demands. And I think it's good that we have some sort of direction here. I've talked to people from other local groups around the city. A lot of energy is being pulled away from groups that normally have a hundred volunteers doing stuff, and now they only have five. So, there does need to be something done with the amount of energy here. Otherwise, projects that have been going on for years and years are going to fall through, all for this to do nothing but come to a big … you know, something should come.

When my friend invited me to come and check it out, before I arrived, I was pretty skeptical. But once I got here, I was surprised at how different it is from most protests. Most protests don't feel as if they're going anywhere in accomplishing anything. As I said, this is like a new city, and it feels like a new world could spring out of it. People are committing their lives to it. They're living down here; they're working seven days a week to make things happen. It's not just an afternoon march along a street. It's twenty-four hours a day, seven days a week, till we get what we want.

We've hit rock bottom in this country, and a lot of people here don't have anywhere else to go. So they're just going to remain here and keep working together until something changes.

RC: Is there a core issue for you? If you had to put your finger on one core issue, what would it be?

SB: I feel that the rich who live or work in the buildings around us should give their money to the people in taxes, or in some form, to make sure that we at least have the basic standards that every human being should have.

RC: When you say "rich," do you mean the top one percent? Or are you talking about people making over $250,000 a year?

SB: For the sake of being here, I'd say, yes, the top one percent definitely needs to give something. But I mean, my parents are upper middle class. They're not necessarily in the top one percent. But they could do more, that's for sure.

RC: One of the young men I spoke with who works in the audio-visual group said that he came out of a Mormon background. Eventually he rejected it, but he kept a sense of direct individual spiritual experience: not an institutional, church type of spirituality. He feels that one of the special things about this generation and the people in this protest is that many have lost a sense of meaning. But now, this event in particular is offering a sense of meaning to many in your generation. Otherwise, all they're offered is a culture that encourages narcissism, apathy, a lack of empathy, and a cause-and-effect way of looking at the world rather than a more meaningful experience, such as art offers, for example. Do you feel anything similar to that?

SB: I do. When I came down here, the first big thing I felt was: happy that people weren't just watching TV, or playing video games, or doing something isolated, alone in a room. Everyone my age has spent so much time isolated, alone in a room, in a self-created prison of sorts. And it's nice to be out, meeting all sorts of people and learning new ideas. I've probably learned more this week than I did during a year in college. It's really a beautiful, amazing thing.

RC: That's one of the great ironies of the Internet: the so-called Web. People talk about social networking, connectivity, being connected, getting connected. But so much of it is sitting alone in a room under the blue "moonlight" of your monitor, being stuck like a fly on a web, and being cut off from others. But you feel that perhaps this is an antidote to all that.

SB: Yes.

* * *

Jenny was conspicuous in her canary-yellow "Grandmothers for Peace" apron. After she took a break from her marching, we spoke about the future of the movement.

RC: Have you been down here since the beginning?

Jenny: Some of us were, a group of about fifteen was here since the first day. Three members were arrested at the Union Square rally, and others have been arrested at various other times. We feel very strongly about supporting Occupy Wall Street and about how our messages are the same.

RC: What are your impressions of the young people here?

Jenny: I'm so impressed by the energy, the thoughtfulness, and the commitment not just to goals but, even more so, to a paradigm shift around communication and discourse. There are any number of people here who are not on the same wavelength as I am. I mean, I'm not a Libertarian; I'm not particularly into waving American flags, or anything like that. But the fact is, their commitment is to deepening discourse and to not polarizing.

When there's a police action that is brutal – and they've been awful – the commitment after addressing what's happened is: "Let's get back on focus." The other day, we were yelling, "You are the ninety-nine percent!" to the cops. That's a really significant thing to be supporting. When we hear antipolice comments, we can talk about "abuse is abuse," but there are still individual police officers who are operating without contact who are part of us.

RC: A year from now, ten years from now, how will people talk about what's happened here?

Jenny: I don't think the change is going to be in my lifetime or in your lifetime. But hopefully the discourse will change over time.

RC: Anything you'd like to add?

Jenny: This is an amazing, wonderful experience, and we need to guard against it being co-opted. The other day, someone said, "Oh, it's too bad there isn't a centralized group with a message." And I almost had a heart attack. I said the strength of this is that it *isn't* that. Any push toward centralization or toward a hierarchal model is in total opposition to what the strength of this is about.

In terms of real change, I don't think we're going to see things in our lifetime. But now there's a different model out there; that's what's critical. And I believe that will continue.

RC: It's also educating a lot of people. As it seeps into the middle class, they'll be thinking about some of these things for the first time.

Jenny: Yes. And there are people from all over the country here. There are even kids from Kentucky who came to study the model. They came for twenty-four hours, to sleep here and to study it. Next week, they'll be starting an "Occupy Lexington, Kentucky."

RC: I saw on the Internet that there's even an Occupy North Dakota!

Jenny: Yes!

RC: So I thought, that's got to mean something.

Jenny: That's right.

* * *

I briefly joined a group of three union members, each about fifty years old, who were sitting at the southeastern edge of the park. Pete and Dave are Teamsters who work at Sotheby's; Rob is a member of the Ironworkers Union.

RC: Why are you guys here today?

Rob: I've been waiting for this for the last three years. Ever since the bailouts in 2008 I've been angry, and I've been waiting for something to pop up, and now it's popping up.

RC: What union are you with?

Rob: Ironworkers.

RC: And what about you?

Dave: Teamsters.

RC: I remember growing up in the Sixties. Every night at the dinner table, we saw a list of the boys who were killed in Vietnam and the towns that they were from.

Dave: Yes. I'm fifty years old; I remember that.

RC: When the body bags returned to the middle class, that's when the bulk of the country got behind ending the war, because it was affecting the middle class.

Dave: They shut that down now. You don't even know what's going on. It's not in the news. You can't see the bodies.

RC: Ever since the Iraq War, it's been against the law for journalists to photograph the coffins draped with flags.

Dave: Right.

RC: I went on a rally with the protestors on October 5. I came because the Transit Workers and other unions were here. And I mentioned to some of these kids that in the Sixties and Seventies it wasn't the same. There were images of construction workers …

Rob: Yes, the hard-hat riots happened right there – two blocks away. I believe they were building the Trade Center.

RC: So you guys know what I'm leading to: the workers beating up the protestors and so on. The unions got behind the students in May 1968 in Paris and they almost brought down the government, but it never happened here. This is an extraordinary story, that we have unions and students, younger people and older people, all working together. What do you guys think about that? Am I correct?

Dave: Absolutely. For years, in the union movement, we've been talking to our members about what was coming their way. We've been telling our guys about all the little things that happened in the shop, and the cutbacks they wanted to make, and the tweaking of the language, and messing with the contract.

They're kind of asleep; it's hard to wake them up and to

get them to hear. But now it's actually happening, and people everywhere are understanding it. The labor unions have been talking about it for years, so it's not new to us.

To specifically answer your question: look at us. We're Teamsters, and we work at Sotheby's. I think you heard about that; we've been locked out. So, one of the very first things that happened during Occupy Wall Street is that some of these people, they knew about it somehow, and they came up there and went into the auction room and made a disruption. That's how we became aware of this. Then we decided to come down and support them.

RC: When that happened, what was your reaction?

Dave: The guys thought it was great.

RC: Why is it that you guys, and your fellow union members, have a different perspective about the protestors than the workers did in the 1960s?

Rob: The thing that caused the split with the blue-collar workers in the Sixties was all kinds of social stuff like long hair, rock'n'roll, and drugs. But now, that's all become part of the culture; that's accepted by almost everybody. To have someone with long hair isn't shocking anymore. Half the construction workers have tattoos and look like freaks. So, that's been put behind us. And maybe we're all getting together on the same page on the important issue, which is making the system work for everybody.

An Interview with William Scott, Author of *Trouble-makers: Power, Representation, and the Fiction of the Mass Worker**

At the northeastern edge of Liberty Plaza I encountered a youthful-looking man in his early forties who was sitting on the ground, handing out flyers advertising his book. When I read the title, Troublemakers: Power, Representation, and the Fiction of the Mass Worker, *I sat down and conducted this impromptu interview.*

William Scott is an associate professor of English at the University of Pittsburgh. He's been sleeping in the park beside the other demonstrators since he first arrived on 6 October. A few days after our talk, he began to work at the "People's Library" as a volunteer. Troublemakers, *published by Rutgers University Press, is his first book.*

Rob Couteau: What's your book about?

William Scott: It's about the way novelists portrayed mass-worker movements in the first half of the twentieth century. When I say mass workers, I mean workers in mass-production industries such as auto and steel, on assembly lines.

In part, it's also about a new form of power that mass workers discovered they had: one that didn't depend on union representation or political party representation. It was a power they derived not so much through the power of numbers but through their position at the workplace, on the assembly line. That is, when ten workers discovered that if they stopped work they could shut down a whole factory if they sat down, that was an enormous power that workers discovered.

This new form of power created a crisis for novelists

who tried to represent mass-worker movements. What they were trying to do was to show that mass workers in their oppressed conditions on assembly lines actually did have a form of power that was not the conventional form that was popular in the nineteenth century – power through representation, power through political parties in unions – but rather that they had a kind of structural or material power from the workplace itself. And so, my book is about how novelists represented this new kind of worker and this new form of power. I talk about novels that tried to detail sit-down strikes, or acts of spontaneous sabotage, or, in general, direct action: direct democracy movements in mass-industrial settings.

RC: How long have you been teaching?

WS: For about eight years. I was at New Mexico University at Las Cruces for about two years, in the English department there. I've been at Pittsburgh for six years.

RC: How long did you work on the book?

WS: On and off, for about ten years.

RC: Who are the writers that you focus on? What's the main group?

WS: The most well known writers that I discuss are people like Upton Sinclair, Jack London, and Dalton Trumbo: those are some of the better-known writers. The rest of them have fallen into obscurity. When their books were initially published though, many of them were bestsellers. Some of the novels I talk about from the progressive era – the period of World War One – were bestsellers and were well known but have fallen into obscurity since then. One of the purposes of the book is to revive attention on these forgotten novels.

RC: You mentioned Dalton Trumbo …

WS: Trumbo's novel, *Johnny Got His Gun*, was a controversial, famous antiwar novel from 1939, and I talk about that in the book.

RC: I forgive myself for not recognizing his name at first, because it's one of those examples of where the book title is more famous than the author.

WS: It is. They made of film of it, as well.* It was a very popular book, used for a sort of peace propaganda: an antiwar, pacifist propaganda novel.

RC: Maybe you could mention some of the books and authors that have fallen into obscurity that you're trying to highlight.

WS: One terrific novel from 1939 that's out of print is by a woman named Ruth McKenney. It's about the Akron rubber workers, the tire workers, and their sit-down strikes in the 1930s. Cornell University Press reprinted it in the early Nineties, but it's been out of print for about twenty years. I would love to see that book put out again. It's a fantastic novel. I have a lot to say about it.

Then there's Thomas Bell, author of a novel called *Out of This Furnace*, which is actually well-known in Pennsylvania and around the Pittsburgh region. It's about the Pittsburgh Steel workers. That's still in print, but it's not very well known. Then there are a bunch of novels from the progressive era, writers who were affiliated with the Industrial Workers of the World: Leroy Scott, author of *The Walking Delegate*; another book by a guy named Ernest Poole, called *The Harbor*, about dock workers and harbor workers in the New York harbor. A wonderful book. Then a book by a guy named Arthur Bullard called *Comrade Yetta*, from 1913, about textile workers in New York: shirtwaist workers and that kind of stuff. Those are a few of them. The list goes on, and there are other novels that I could mention.

RC: How did the idea for this generate? Where did you get the idea?

WS: My doctoral dissertation and research was about leftist writers from the Great Depression. In the course of doing this research, I discovered there was a broader tradition of radical literature in this country. So, I wanted to do something that would be broader than just a focus on the 1930s. That's pretty much the origin of it.

RC: What gave you the idea of doing the dissertation originally?

WS: When I was in graduate school, I was interested in the history of U.S. social movements. I was in a comparative lit program, so I started off studying German literature and German philosophy, that sort of thing. Then I discovered there was a movement of radical writers, leftist writers, in the Depression. I had no idea who these authors were. The only writers I ever knew from the 1930s were people like Hemingway, Steinbeck, *The Grapes of Wrath*. But to learn that there was a whole movement that was organized, that had conferences, journals, magazines, and published all sorts of stories, poems, plays, and novels from this era: that just blew my mind. I decided I wanted to learn more about it and that it would be a good topic: an under-researched field, which needed to be looked at again.

RC: You discuss major authors, such as Upton Sinclair, who explore this theme as a focal point in their work. But do you also mention writers that we don't necessarily associate with this theme but who were, nonetheless, affected by it and who dramatized it to some extent?

WS: Pretty much all the novelists I discuss were authors who had a commitment to writing about class issues and the situation of the working class. So, it's hard for me to think of writers who took up that intent as a sort of peripheral or secondary kind of thing. John Steinbeck would be a good example. I don't write about him in the book. But he's a good example of someone who has a sort of side interest in workers' movements in this country, and he addressed it in some of his novels. *The Grapes of Wrath* is the most famous one. Maybe Dalton Trumbo is the most famous example of somebody. *Johnny Got His Gun* is not typically thought of as a book about workers. But in the novel, it's clear that the main character is there to be a typical example of a modern mass-industrial worker. Jack London is another writer who was personally a socialist and was involved with the Socialist Party. He didn't write a lot about workers, though, except in a few of his books. Maybe he's another good example of somebody like that.

RC: Jack London brings a lot of those issues to the fore in his quasi-autobiographical novel, *Martin Eden.*

WS: Oh, *Martin Eden*! Absolutely!

RC: That's an amazing book, isn't it?

WS: Yes! I don't write about it in my book; I write about *The Iron Heel* a little bit, which was a very popular book. And *Martin Eden* was, too; they were both popular books with progressives and with labor activists in the progressive era. For example, he was one of the favorite authors of the Wobblies: the IWW. In many ways, *The Iron Heel* was a prophetic book. It's a fantastic novel.

RC: You could say that many of his tales and stories that have to do with going to exotic places – such as to Alaska, for the Gold Rush – are about people who are *working*, trying to make money.

WS: Absolutely. Then there are his allegorical stories, as well. Even the stories about animals are often allegorical tales about human society.

Historians and sociologists will tell you that this era we're living in now, of big corporate capital, most resembles the period of the 1890s in America: the Gilded Age, the creation of monopoly capital. Big trusts, and things like that. It's the kind of capitalism that Jack London was trying to describe in his books. For that reason, I think he's a very contemporary writer, and the things he says are relevant to many of the struggles that people are having today.

RC: I recently interviewed Justin Kaplan, who won a Pulitzer Prize for his biography on Mark Twain. We were talking about Twain, Whitman, and the Gilded Age, and we touched on the fact that, yes, there really is a connection from that period to this period. Especially when I read about Whitman's life, I see some amazing connections. The 1850s was a decade that one could easily compare to the 1960s: a time of eccentric personal fashion and culture. And then, proceeding into the 1890s, there's a palpable disgust with the growing power of corporations and how the law was no longer equally applied between a citizen and a plutocrat.

WS: Yes.

RC: So, there's certainly a parallel. Which leads us to the fact that there are *cycles* that we see throughout history.

WS: Oh, yes, that's true. In part, one of the reasons there are cycles is because, relatively speaking, Americans are less history conscious as compared with people in Europe. I studied in Germany; I lived there for a while, and I followed the German news. On historical memorial days when they have these milestones, these anniversaries, they're presented as major news stories. We rarely see that in our news here. You can grow up watching the news – if you even watch the news in this country – and never learn about American history. In this country, the news usually focuses on the present.

In general, with Americans, part of their identity is to be always forward looking: gazing into the future and not looking back. This goes part and parcel with the ideology of American identity.

RC: There's a reason for that, because this country attracted immigrants from other places.

WS: Exactly.

RC: At that time, in the nineteenth century, to take a big boat trip like that, you certainly had to have a lot of optimism about the future. You had to be a gambler; you had to be a bit of an intuitive: to believe in possibilities rather than actualities.

WS: Right.

RC: That's the filter through which the American character has been formed.

WS: Yes, absolutely. But I think the downside is that we do tend to repeat things. In part, there are cycles because of this almost constitutional amnesia.

RC: We forget about the past.

WS: We forget about the past, and then the past repeats itself. Vietnam is a wonderful example, a timely example. I'm a big fan of the history of the Vietnam War; I'm very interested in it. I'm fascinated by the various ways that it was debated and the ways it was resisted: all those kinds of things. Also by the rationale, the motivation that was used to get us in the war and to keep us in the war for all that time.

If you look at the arguments that were made, and the mission of the U.S. military in Vietnam, almost point for point it matches up with Afghanistan. Not so much with Iraq, but with Afghanistan. That is, you have a mountainous region, nomadic peoples, and our mission is to spread not just democracy but to spread a kind of service: a "goodwill mission," right? But it's a war, nonetheless. When you hear pundits denying the similarities between Vietnam and Afghanistan, I think they have to do that to distract attention away from the glaring parallels and similarities.

I grew up watching movies like *The Deer Hunter*, *Apocalypse Now*: all these movies that were critical of U.S. involvement in Vietnam. And I grew up naively thinking, well, with films like this, we'll never have to worry about another Vietnam, because everyone knows why it's wrong and what's wrong with these kinds of wars. With any war, but with these in particular. Yet, it started all over again, ten years ago.

RC: The powers-that-be have a great interest in dumbing down the Americans, and in underfunding education, because they don't want people to know about these things.

WS: Right.

RC: One of the big differences between Vietnam and Afghanistan is that they learned their lesson after allowing the journalists to roam free through the jungles of Vietnam. In Iraq and Afghanistan, they created a policy of so-called embedded journalists: reporters were attached to military units and couldn't wander around, unsupervised. Another difference is that it became unlawful for journalists to photograph the coffins coming back, draped in American flags.

WS: From Afghanistan and Iraq, yes.

RC: There's even more control of the media now than

there was back then. I grew up in the 1960s, watching the TV every night at the dinner table …

WS: The dead bodies …

RC: Yes. During the news, wherever you were in America, you'd see the names of the boys, often from local neighborhoods, who were killed, and where they were from. Largely, these were body bags that came back to the working- and middle class. And because the middle class was affected, that galvanized the antiwar movement and made it a serious threat to the status quo.

The connection between those protests and this one, which we're sitting in the midst of today, is that the middle class are a significant part of the ninety-nine percent. They're directly affected, even though, now, the issue is the economy.

WS: Yes, I totally agree. The other day, there was a woman at the general assembly meeting who was saying that the thing this generation and this particular protest has in common with the antiwar protests in the Sixties is that, in the Sixties, everyone was worried about being drafted. You stayed in college so you wouldn't get drafted. And the way to protest this was to burn your draft card. Everyone knew that they were at risk for dying; they knew people who were dying; they knew they, themselves, were at risk for being sent over there. It was also clear that it was a war against lower-income Americans and people of color. They were the vast majority of the people who were being put on front lines and being killed.

RC: Especially by 1968, toward the end of the war.

WS: Exactly. We don't have a draft today, and the thing about the war in Iraq and in Afghanistan is that the majority of middle-class Americans don't feel directly affected by this. They don't feel as though they're at risk for being sent over and killed. But what we do have today, which students did not have in the Sixties, is student-loan debt. And the easy availability of credit has made it even worse.

When I was an undergraduate at SUNY Buffalo, during my first year on campus, credit companies gave me credit cards and said, "Here, go out and use this." I didn't even have to apply; they gave them to me on the spot, on campus. They had tables set up, and they were handing out credit cards. So, what did I do? I was like, "Hey, I've never had a credit card before. I'll go and buy some CDs." I go and buy some CDs; I'm into debt immediately. This is twenty years ago. Ever since then, I've been struggling with paying off credit-card debt, student-loan debt. I had to pay for my own tuition through college, so I had to take out student loans. I'm still paying that off. Thank God I have a stable job, a good job, and I can pay it. But the situation this puts the vast majority of people in – younger people especially – is that, now, when you're in college, you're racking up debt. So, college is actually not a safe place to be anymore; it's a dangerous thing.

When people graduate with $100,000 in student loans, they have to take that job at Starbucks, and they have to take that job willingly and obediently. They cannot talk back to their supervisors, because they need to keep the job to pay off debt. If they don't, their credit is going to be screwed up, and their lives are going to be screwed up from that point on, and they won't be able to buy a car or a house.

So, this is an interesting parallel. What that woman was asking students to do was to burn their student-loan paperwork. Which, idealistically, sounds wonderful. But, realistically, you're screwing yourself if you do that. I would never have thought to do that myself. But it's true that if every student from today to tomorrow decided to not pay their student loans anymore, and to walk away from it, that would create another kind of crisis.

RC: It may not be the most pragmatic solution, but it's a highly effective dramatic symbolic action, which is very important to have in a movement. I often think of how, in 1967, Abbie Hoffman and the Yippies, and Allen Ginsberg, and so many other groups went down to Washington with the intention of levitating the Pentagon through yoga meditation and by chanting, "Out, demon, out!" [Laughs] The Pentagon building is shaped like a five-pointed star, so they thought it was akin to a black-magic pentagram. And this event still resonates among contemporary historians of this period. Norman Mailer's book, *The Armies of the Night*, is about that same protest. So, these symbolic acts are very important. Burning a draft card is an image that resonates, that stays in people's minds. Back then, people would have seen it in *Life* magazine. It's a provocation, an important provocation.

WS: Absolutely, I agree. If you want to see a parallel between this kind of action and that Pentagon action, you're right to see it in these protests as well. Although, in some ways, the focus of the energy at this event, and at similar events that are happening around the country and springing up spontaneously in different cities, has a kind of focus, in spite of the fact that there are no clear demands or concrete sound-bite demands. The focus on finance capital is something that is extremely powerful and that was missing from the Sixties generation, which was mainly engaged in antiwar protest. To some degree, there was a critique of capitalism in there, as well. The problem in the Sixties was that there were competing leftist ideologies. You had Maoists fighting with communists and this kind of thing. We were still in the Cold War period, so communism became a banner under which people were organized, but it was a controversial one.

What's great about this event is that it's relatively free from limited political or ideological definitions or categories. This is really a bonus. Yet, it doesn't lose its main focus on finance capitalism, on corporate capitalism.

RC: Why are you here today?

WS: I have a sabbatical this semester; I don't have to teach. When I first started hearing about this, I thought: This is really important; I want to support it. Luckily, I don't have to teach classes now, so I'm here supporting it.

RC: Considering what your book is about, this is the perfect question to ask. In America in the Sixties and early Seventies, the unions never aligned with the students.

WS: Right.

RC: A few blocks from this location, an event happened in the early 1970s that was photographed and widely reproduced. Construction workers attacked the youth movement as they were marching in protest: violently attacked them, beat some of them to a pulp. And now, we've got major unions, such as the U.S. Steelworkers and the Transit Workers Union, joining a largely youthful protest movement at the beginning, after just a few weeks. What's the significance of that to you?

WS: That is huge. That is actually the secret of May 1968 in Paris. A short-lived kind of success, but, nevertheless, a significant coalition. This is what we didn't have in the U.S. in '68. Instead, there was a lot of tension between organized labor and the antiwar movement.

That's a complicated issue, which has a lot of factors involved in explaining why that's so. It took forty years for organized labor to realize that they were getting shafted. In the Sixties, that process had just started; it hadn't yet kicked in. Mass workers and unions were incredibly strong and still had a lot to gain. The industrialization and outsourcing hadn't hit home yet to the industrial workers in this country. Forty years later, it's hit home in a major way. We've seen outsourcing and the export of an industrial economy out of this country. So, for many years, unions have been in the doldrums and have, in some ways, needed something like this to give them the sort of push they needed to speak out about it.

RC: It's easy to understand why, in May '68, the unions in Paris had an almost instant solidarity with the students, because there's more of a history of that kind of thing there. When there's a strike in France, it often leads to a domino effect.

WS: Yes.

RC: Why do you think it took so long for workers here to understand the need to create this coalition? Why do you think they attacked the students then, and they're not doing it now? What's changed?

WS: I think it's because, in the history of our country, the work ethic is extremely important. In the U.S. we live in culture that worships work for its own sake and that worships work for the sake of upward mobility. The American dream is about working hard and moving up. But there's also a religious element to it: a Puritan work ethic. To be a good American, you have to work hard.

The tension between the student movement and labor existed throughout the 1960s. Hippies were called "bums." They were "lazy bums" and, supposedly, they didn't work. And so, what "hippy" stood for was an anti-work ethic. This made them very unpopular with organized labor.

The reason it took so long is because of the persistence and resilience of the work ethic: this never goes away. Even among the Left and people who are sort of "pro-working class," there's almost a fetishization of working for its own sake: the value of work.

What you're seeing now among working people and organized labor is a convergence of frustration with the economy, with Wall Street, with Congress, and with the outsourcing of jobs. It's a dovetailing of that frustration with the anxiety of the student generation, who can't find work and who need to find work to pay off student-loan debt. These two things are coming together, and it's happening right now. That's one theory I would have to explain why, now, there's a compatibility. And organized labor has finally woken up to realize that it's OK to be critical of the American work ethic in some ways.

RC: We're each a little older than many of the people in this crowd. Especially with the teenagers that I speak to, they really believe in their hearts that something fundamental is about to change. But you and I know how deeply corrupt this country is, and all governments in the world are, and what a dark network exists between governments, major corporations, organized crime, international narcotraffickers: all of that. That's the real "worldwide web." Bearing this in mind, where do you think this is going to go? Where's it going to be a year from now? How are people going to look back on this, twenty or thirty years from now? Are these kids going to be disappointed when the fundamentals don't instantly transform?

WS: Honestly, I can't tell yet. I would be uncomfortable making predictions about that. One side of me, the cynical side, sees all this getting burned out as soon as the weather gets cold and everyone goes home. Then it will be a blip on the radar of the popular cultural history of the United States, and nothing more. But another part of me, the less cynical, more optimistic, hopeful side, thinks that even if the momentum of this particular action trails away, others will take its place. That it will start a domino effect that we haven't seen in our country for a long time. That could be really positive. So, I don't know.

A year from now, what I would love to see is for politicians to actually try to respond to these kinds of demands. Just in the last two years, you've seen the political response, directly, to the Tea Party actions around the country. A very organized movement, and they were directly responded to. They had leverage in the last election, and they will have leverage in the next election. If a similar kind of thing from a progressive point of view could have the same kind of leverage, that could help to balance the scales a bit.

Because of the direction this country's been moving in the last few years, and particularly with the rise of the Tea Party, I've been really frightened, you know? When I hear the Republican nominees, it's really frightening, the kinds of things I hear them say and the kind of things I know they would be supporting. So, if nothing else, even if this fizzled out next week, it could still have the potential to exert some influence in electoral politics.

A lot of people that you'll speak to here are against electoral politics completely. They think the whole system is completely corrupt. And that's a valid position to have. Representational democracy *is* incredibly corrupt, especially when corporations are considered people and they can vote, and they can donate as much as they want to campaigns. This makes everyone here very skeptical.

RC: Talk about a symbolically significant image – a corporation as a person!

WS: Absolutely. That captures the essence of something that's so upsetting to people here.

RC: In fact, corporations *have* become people, because the government's allowed for it. I mean, they have become people in the sense of having personal rights. Even more than people: like "superpeople."

WS: Yes. That's why I think it's valid for a lot of people here not to want to participate in electoral politics. That's fine, but if Sarah Palin is our next president because they didn't go out and vote, they'll only have themselves to blame!* So, I think it's right to critique the system of electoral representation and democracy, but you work with what you've got.

RC: Both things are important: voting, as well as taking to the streets. And right now, taking to the streets is a very meaningful thing to do.

WS: Yes. About a hundred years ago, there was a very similar debate in this country about the value of electoral representation. The Socialist Party was pushing for Eugene Debs to get a lot of votes and to become president. Campaign after campaign, he kept running for president, and he kept getting more and more votes. Upton Sinclair talks about it in *The Jungle*. But there was another sphere of labor people and activists who said this was all a waste of time. The Industrial Workers of the World were competing against that system of democracy. They felt we needed a direct democracy or a worker's democracy. A democracy that would become a reality through the direct action of workers.

In many ways, the reason why this protest appeals to me

so much and interests me so much is that I see this as a version of that. Just people realizing a new form of democracy.

RC: In the decades before television, even for those who weren't necessarily interested in literary things per se, there were often books in the household, as a form of entertainment. But with the advent of television, the novel became less influential in the United States. One of the indications of this is that organizations such as the CIA spent increasingly less time, money, and energy on infiltrating literary magazines and literary groups, and on keeping tabs on authors, and things like that. Instead, the film stars and other celebrities were monitored, because they had so much more power. For example, a movie star could call a press conference and draw instant headlines.

In some interview, there's an apt quote by the playwright Arthur Miller. Just before he was due to testify at the House Un-American Activities Committee, he received a message from the one of the congressmen in charge of the hearings. He told Miller: If Marilyn Monroe would just pose in a photo with me, I'd be willing to drop the whole thing. Miller later said that it resembled the cathartic moment in a play: the emotional focal point in which everything is symbolized in one quintessential gesture. He added that the significance of this was that they weren't calling lowly secretaries and bureaucrats from the American Communist Party to testify; they were calling Hollywood celebrities, because that was the only way to maintain headlines.

Bearing all this in mind, what is the political role of the novelist today?

WS: I would hesitate to spell out any particular criteria for things that writers ought to be writing about. In part, I say this as a result of my own research in looking at the debate around the role of the writer in the Thirties, during the Great Depression. There were huge debates about what writers should be doing during this crisis.

RC: That's a good point; let me rephrase the question. What is the role of a politically motivated writer, such as Upton Sinclair and those other well-known novelists that you talk about? What role could they play today? I'm not necessarily asking, "What role *should* they play?" but I'm asking "what role *can* they play" in the context of the background I just gave you?

WS: It's important for people to be aware of them for a number of reasons, and to be aware of the way that politics gets worked out through literature in this country: with all it's mistakes, with all its blind spots. It's important to see how this process works and unfolds, and for people to understand that it's possible to be a writer, and do very creative work, and still have political convictions, and to not see an incompatibility between these two things. John Reed, the writer that Warren Beatty portrayed in the film *Reds*, was also very famous for one of the last statements he made, supposedly on his deathbed. He said, "It's a hell of a thing, trying to juggle poetry and politics." You know, the idea that revolution and poetry never go hand in hand.

The assumption that there's an inherent conflict between poetry and politics is something that, for a long time, writers have dealt with or have tried to work in the shadow of. I think it's important for writers, and for people today, students of literature, to understand that there's never been a huge conflict between creative work and political work. The two have always gone hand in hand, going back to the eighteenth century even. And that you don't have to write an overtly political poem or novel for that to be a valid expression of your politics.

Right now, I see a lot of potential, particularly in poetry and politics. The reason I say this is because poetry – and this has always been true of poetry – has been an easier genre for people to make their lives heard in: for people who are not trained as writers to throw something together. For example, workers have often written poems. With the slam poetry movement, which emerged about ten, fifteen years ago, that had – and still has – a lot of potential to be used for consciousness raising and for political awareness. Hip-hop has obviously gotten a lot of attention for its political potential. Talib Kweli, a contemporary hip-hop artist, was here a couple of nights ago as a guest, and he did some songs. It was obvious to everyone why he wanted to be here, and why he wanted to perform for us. It was really profound, the kind of message he was providing.

RC: You brought up an interesting point just now about the fact that the two don't have to contradict each other. Jim Feast, who's a critic for the *Evergreen Review*, has been doing an ongoing series about how the most significant writers are never writing out of a vacuum. They're not just portraying themselves in a kind of cerebral cubicle, cut off from the rest of society. Instead, the really great writers are always portraying something that reflects the larger society, the major currents, the historical trend, the overall picture of the moment. Do you agree?

WS: I do, although I don't think they're always conscious of doing that. A very well known Marxist literary critic who teaches at Duke University, Fredric Jameson, wrote an influential book in the early 1980s called *The Political Unconscious*. His argument is that writers, whether they know it or not, are always responding to the political and social issues of their time. The work that they're doing is shaped by this, and it's always a response, whether it's conscious or unconscious. He uses the analogy of dreams, Freud's theory of dreams, that our dreams are always a wish fulfillment. Jameson thought that we should see literature as expressing a kind of wish fulfillment for some type of political solution or change in our society. I think there's a lot to be said for this type of approach.

RC: Of course, if dreams were wish fulfillment, we'd never have nightmares! But that's a long discussion.

WS: Freud actually has a lot to say about nightmares.

RC: I know, he's got an excuse for everything!

WS: [Laughs]

RC: On the opposite side of the spectrum, we also have authors such as John Reed who are so one-sidedly obsessed with the notion of changing the world, and obsessed with their own political advocacy role, that, sometimes, we have to question whether there's something more personal at work that's being projected upon this whole screen. For instance, in *Reds*, a marvelous film that touches on a lot of these things, the director Warren Beatty features several interviews with Henry Miller. There's a classic quote where Miller says: "Yeah, John Reed, he was a real rabble-rouser, a troublemaker. The problem with him was that he wanted to change the world. And nobody can change the world, not even Jesus Christ. Look at what they did to him; they crucified the poor bastard!" Then he ends the quote by saying: "When you're that obsessed with wanting to change the world, we have to question whether there's really something inside yourself that needs change." A valid point?

WS: Well, yes, that's a valid point. But it doesn't invalidate the kinds of commitments and values that somebody like John Reed had, and the things he was trying to do. There's always a psychopathological or neurotic explanation for what everybody does.

RC: We're motivated by many things …

WS: Yes.

RC: Most of them beyond the analysis of a Freud or a Jung anyway.

WS: Yes. And apart from college debt, one thing that probably the majority of the people here have in common is that their mothers didn't love them enough! [Laughs] I mean, you could probably make that prediction. Or they had some other familial issue that made them turn to issues of social justice and see a lot of hope in that. But that doesn't discount or discredit the fact that they're still trying to do something positive to make the world a better place.

RC: Yes, indeed. Thanks so much for talking with me today.

WS: Thank you!

---

* This interview was conducted on 8 October 2011.

* In 1971, *Johnny Got His Gun* was made into a film directed by Dalton Trumbo. It was remade in 2008 and directed by Rowan Joseph.

* In 2008, Sarah Palin ran as the Republican vice-presidential candidate.

ALSO BY ROB COUTEAU

THE SLEEPING MERMAID

Novelist and literary enthusiast Rob Couteau brings readers part of his love with *The Sleeping Mermaid*, a book of flowing poetry and thought that asks plenty of questions and offers plenty of answers. *The Sleeping Mermaid* is a poetry collection well-worth considering.
– Willis M. Buhle, *Midwest Book Review.*

Had Henry Miller written poetry it might have resembled the poems of Robert Couteau you are about to read (or have read, and have come to me afterwards, as you probably should). This is not to imply that Couteau is a Miller knock-off. He's not. He's an American original, as was Miller. What I mean is simply that Couteau, with his painter's eye (another Miller similarity), addresses quite directly themes and subjects that Miller was also enamored by: Paris, women, the quotidian surprises life throws us, an acute understanding of mythology and folktale, of tradition and revolution, and finally, the chance encounters that, if we are wise enough to embrace them, help to make us more human.

In Couteau's work there is no phoniness, no artifice for the sake of artifice – though in the great French tradition this poet knows so well, there is some art for the sake of art. Couteau does not venture into realms of obscurity where meaning is confined to the interior of a Klein bottle; his poems all have direct force, subjects, even verbs. He is intent on having his readers share in his observations, whether it be his artful retelling and reinterpretations of

Native American story and song, or his appraisal of how a woman parades across the avenue. He does not ever sacrifice ordinary sense for an extra-ordinary significance. Instead, he speaks with fervor, with something to say, with something he wants us to hang onto and in the process come to an understanding of why it matters not just to him but should matter to us. In other words: he knows what he wants to say, and says it.

Couteau's poetic material is as vast as his learning and imagination. And yet he does not seem overly concerned with making tidy themes, or buttoning his knowledge into a small sphere. Indeed, I often sense that he hasn't really selected his material; rather his material seems to have selected him. But obedient to the muse and his own gifts, he records for us with clear-eyed insight the spectrum of his collisions between subject and object, the real and imagined, the read and reread and then reinvented, himself and the perceived, the distillate of being always awake and attentive to what confronts him. Indeed. Couteau is not conditional in his probing of the human condition, even to the point of exposing his own condition in face of what he is examining. He steps right in, and in turn allows us the gift of his informed vision. What we see is not always pretty, nor dressed up for the photo-op. But he never panders. He sees what he sees and puts it down on the page with grace and often beauty. And we, as readers, benefit enormously for his willingness to go the distance with what matters.

I think it was William Carlos Williams who said that poetry is belief. Couteau believes in belief, believes that poetic worth is measured in faithfulness to what is, what has been, and what could be. These are his talismans; these are the points where he begins and ends. His poetic excursions take us to many places: to the Paris of Rimbaud and

Picasso, to the Native North Americans, to mythology and history and how the woman he is encountering is seducing him as he seduces her (and us), and finally, how alone, the cosmos plays itself out at 3 a.m. when the only lap dog is memory.

– A former creative-writing teacher at MIT, Christopher Sawyer-Lauçanno is the author of *The Continual Pilgrimage: American Writers in Paris, 1944-1960, E. E. Cummings*, and *An Invisible Spectator, A Biography of Paul Bowles*.

DOCTOR PLUSS, WITH AN AFTERWARD BY JIM FEAST

Reading *Doctor Pluss*, Rob Couteau's intense, dramatic story of a psychologist who works at the Walt Whitman Asylum for Adults, one might think, especially since there is no authorial information given on the book, that Couteau is a psychiatrist of some sort. How else could he write with such assurance about this milieu?

However, turning to his book of essays, poems, reviews, and interviews, *Collected Couteau*, though it, too, contains no authorial information, one begins to see that he is a well-informed layman who has thought deeply about psychological issues. Not only has he thought, but he has also forged a coherent philosophy through both the direct study of the subject and a close reading of literature.

Part of his philosophy is revealed in the interpretation of schizophrenia in a review of a book by John Perry. He notes that "Perry's work in traditional psychiatric settings led him to conclude that those in the thrall of an acute psychotic episode are rarely listened to or met on the level of their visionary state of consciousness." If care providers paid heed to what the patients were trying to show in their symptoms and musings, they would often find that "forced to live an emotionally impoverished life, the psyche had reacted by provoking a transformation in the form of a 'compensating' psychosis, during which a drama in depth was enacted, forcing the initiate to undergo certain developmental processes."

Couteau quotes Perry concerning this state: "The individual [patient] finds himself living in a psychic modality quite different from his surroundings. He is immersed in a myth world." This modality may seem to be regressive, but it is far from unfruitful. "Although the [myth] imagery is of a general, archetypal nature," writes Couteau, "it also symbolizes the key issues of the individual undergoing the crisis. Therefore, once lived through on this mythic plane, and once the process of withdrawal nears its end, the images must be linked to specific problems of daily life." This leads, in the best cases, to a healing whereby the patient is now able to face and cope with problems that caused the flight into illness.

Perry's work is not that well known, but readers may be more familiar with the once celebrated theories of R. D. Laing. While not finding archetypes in his patients' thoughts, Laing agreed with Perry in treating the schizophrenics' attempts to communicate as valid efforts to reach out, and in finding that their psychological difficulties were often rooted in their untenable lives.

This is not to say that Couteau wholeheartedly endorses these ideas of Perry's. That's not the point. Rather, Dr. Pluss, the staff psychiatrist in the novel named after him, does. Instead of coldly and clinically assessing his schizophrenic patients (as dominant psychiatric norms dictate he should), Pluss befriends them, sharing his own passions, such as his love of modernist art, particularly of Paul Klee, in a workshop where the inmates learn to appreciate art as a form of therapy. Further, he listens carefully to them as they exhaustively recount their life views. He may criticize these patients' sometimes outrageous ideas, but he takes them seriously.

The description on the back of the novel states that the book is "based on actual dialogues with schizophrenic patients," something evident from the stories told to Pluss. With a fantasy akin to Freud's famous Rat Man case, one woman thinks a ravenous cat lives in her midsection. That's why she constantly has to eat. Otherwise, the beast, in its craving for food, will begin consuming her internal organs. (In Freud's story, the patient imagines rats gnawing on his friends' buttocks.)

The most significant patient is Jonah, who believes his own mental problems are so tremendously fascinating that, when he engages in a self-analysis (talking to himself), somehow the Viennese master himself comes back to life to eavesdrop. As Jonah tells Dr. Pluss, "And Freud listened to the analysis, glued to his television. He wouldn't eat; he wouldn't sleep; he wouldn't anything." Ironically enough, Jonah's psychoanalysis simply consists of enumerating, without explaining, his own situation. "I'm a patient; this is a hospital. Why am I in a cage?" While this fantasy may not seem terrifically engaging, when not raving Jonah presents thoughtful and provocative comments on religion, other patients, and even on Dr. Pluss, who is himself undergoing a nervous breakdown.

Pluss had been a painter but gave up the arts to devote himself to helping people. Now, as he is increasingly enthralled by some of his patients' mythic visions, he begins painting again. Using notes of his talks with schizophrenics, he recasts their ideas as art. He creates, for instance, a series of paintings on Jonah, who sometimes thinks of his mind as a clockwork. Pluss depicts "Jonah being cured of paranoia at the Bulova Watch Repair School and leaving behind his persecution complex in the grim milieu of the Bulova assembly line."

Couteau has some misgivings about the sympathetic-ear approach of Perry. This is suggested by the fact that Pluss goes beyond listening to his patients' stories, gets caught up by them, and eventually seems to go a little mad himself when he quits the sanitarium and disappears. I say "seems" because, mirroring Pluss's dissolution, the narrative strands of the book, which had been tightly wound in the first section that focused closely on Pluss, begin to unravel, with Jonah taking over much of the narrative and becoming a new focal point. This shift of gears can be a bit disorienting as the realism of the opening is partially abandoned, but it does give the reader a chance to see the schizophrenia developing as it gains hold of Pluss's thought processes. Pluss is like the psychiatrist Dr. Dysart in Peter Shaffer's play *Equus*, who begins to doubt his profession, since when a cure succeeded, it often converted a passionate, inspired, if addled person into a normal but dull zombie. Pluss is attracted by the crazed creativity of so many of his charges. Unlike Dysart, though, who confines his admiration to rueful ruminations, Pluss mimics his patients, becoming psychotic in the process.

I mentioned previously that Couteau obtained psychological knowledge not only from studying and from thinking about books on the mind but also by reading literature. Indeed, it is important to note that while Pluss took the ultimately dangerous path of learning from his patients, Couteau has deepened his insights by interviewing great writers, such as Ray Bradbury and Hubert Selby Jr.

These interviews are not simple Q&A's but are interactions with a lot of give and take. The interview with Selby (done for *Rain Taxi*) delves deeply into spirituality and ethics. In a notable passage, Selby remarks, "What we seem to be taught, at least in the Western world, is that we're born with a blank slate, and we have to learn how to get and get.... But no one ever seems to train us in methods of finding out that we already have within us all the things that are valuable: all the treasures. But it's only in the process of giving them away, to somebody else, that we become aware of having them."

This thought seems to follow up on insights brought to bear in *Doctor Pluss*. One reason for the immobilization of so many in psychiatric offices or institutions (according to Couteau and the Shaffer of *Equus*) is that conventional education does not provide tools for people to deal with stress or act in a humanitarian, giving manner, only instructing them on how to get ahead.

I can't help, though, but note that Selby, like Couteau, suggests he has learned from unique individuals, pointing to none other than *Evergreen Review's* own editor, Barney Rosset, for special commendation. In discussing his first novel, *Last Exit to Brooklyn*, which Rosset published, Selby engages in an interchange, beginning with Couteau's question:

> Why was *Last Exit* allowed to be published in the United States in 1964, while *Tropic of Cancer*, which was a much less obscene book – by the classical definition – was banned until just a few years before this?
>
> **Selby**: I think because … it [*Tropic*] had been banned for many years. You could only smuggle it in and all that sort of stuff. So, it had a different resistance and a different procedure to go through.
>
> **Couteau**: It had an already established weight, a history that it had to deal with.
>
> **Selby**: Right. Yeah. And, of course, Barney Rosset took care of business and made it possible for a lot of things to happen.

It's nice to see that old debts – Rosset's discovery and championing of Selby's work – are here being repaid, but this also brings me to a final thought on history. Some readers may find Couteau out of date, in that Laing and the antipsychiatry movement to which he belonged are not the household names they were in the 1960s, but they (as represented by Perry) seem to orient and spur the author's fictional and nonfictional excursions. While some may say this current of psychology has been superseded, Couteau has a gone a long way toward showing that it still possesses validity and staying power. How else account for the intellectual freshness, richness, and potency of his novel and essays?

– Jim Feast is the author of *Neo-Phobe* (with Ron Kolm) and the former assistant editor of the *Evergreen Review*.

More Collected Couteau: Essays and Interviews, with an Introduction by James Dempsey

The Renaissance Man is a multi-faceted individual whose fingers are in just about every pie you could imagine, fostering a variety of abilities and mastering many quite well. His expertise is wide-ranging and there's seemingly no limit to his subject, as is demonstrated in *More Collected Couteau: Essays and Interviews*, which gathers Couteau's insights and encounters with a diverse range of individuals.

More Collected Couteau is divided neatly into two segments. The first section of essays probes the anniversary of the publication of *Tropic of Cancer*, the pain and anguish of writer Hubert Selby, and the lasting impact of countercultural icon Jack Kerouac with equal aplomb and vivid imagery.

It doesn't matter if you haven't heard of his subject before, either: take Hubert Selby, for example. Couteau's analysis is striking and revealing: "… the reader is a victim of the greatest and most inhuman assault of all. No matter how monstrous or horrific his depictions of abject brutality are, Selby always ups the ante and makes them worse, pushing the limits until, by the end of the tale, he manages to rape our imagination once again, to puncture yet another hole in our innocence."

The joy of reading Couteau's work lies as much in his penetrating, crystalline language as it does in the works or figures being examined, and so readers receive a wide-ranging treat that examines victims, vengeance, mortality and immortality through an inspection process that educates even those unfamiliar with the subject: "Selby once said: "There is no light in my stories, so the reader is forced to turn to his own inner light" to make it through this journey. I now realize this is only partially true. The great beacon in his demonic oeuvre is that of the artfully crafted line and the immense vision of wholeness and transcendence that lurks behind it. Selby's empathy is there, omnipresent, even while recording the darkest hues of black. The utmost depravity is portrayed with the noblest verse."

After proving his prowess at the essay form, he turns to the heart of the collection: its interviews. These range from discussions with Albert Hoffman (activist and the discoverer of LSD) to interviews with literary figures such as historian and cultural commentator Robert Roper or poet Christopher Sawyer-Lauçanno.

One of the pleasures in this collection is that readers needn't have prior familiarity with the writers' works. Couteau provides that familiarity by the structure of his interview questions, which probe the foundation beliefs of each figure: "The first time I read your wonderful biography, I was struck by how supportive Cummings's father was. After all, he even paid Estlin to write *The Enormous Room*. And I was very thrown off by that. I always thought that artists are supposed to have a contentious relationship with their fathers!"

From the possibility that Nabokov suffered unconscious doubts about his own value that led him to insist that the world acknowledge him as a genius to the underlying patriotism of counterculture icons who were commonly seen as rebels ("Ginsberg continually affirmed that, essentially, Jack had always been a sort of patriotic American," says Sawyer-Lauçanno. "This had never not been part of who he was. It was patriotic to get into an automobile made in Detroit and drive across the country ..."), both essays and interviews are designed to make readers think about underlying psychology, social perceptions, and cultural change.

Readers seeking not just a literary presentation but a lively analysis of selected wordsmiths and their lives and influences must add *More Collected Couteau* to their reading lists. It's a powerful presentation that offers much insight and food for thought, and which should find its way into many a college classroom as well.

– Diane Donovan, *Midwest Book Review.*

Couteau's essays are informal, fervent, and well-versed examinations of the work or author at hand. At their best, they include fascinating insights into the significance of a writer like [Hubert] Selby.... The interviews are uniformly strong and include conversations with Michael Korda on T.E. Lawrence, Justin Kaplan on Walt Whitman, and Robert Roper on Vladimir Nabokov. Not all of them focus on literature: author Jeffrey Jackson covers the 1910 flood of Paris and why it's relatively forgotten, and Robert De Sena, in one of the best interviews, discusses his life as a gang member turned community activist. Couteau's passion and wealth of knowledge are obvious throughout the book ... and should appeal to many readers.

– Publishers Weekly Select.

Good luck trying to pin down Rob Couteau. Name the genre, and Couteau has almost certainly been there and done that. Poet, novelist, essayist, critic, journalist, memoirist, and travel writer, Couteau is not one to be hampered by constraints. He passes easily from one form of literature to another as if the borders between them did not exist for him. Perhaps they don't.

Couteau has been called a "literary enthusiast," and although he certainly is enthusiastic about literature (and indeed all art), the phrase carries the smack of the amateur about it, and Couteau is anything but. He is, in fact, an undeniably consummate professional. He is an independent scholar in every meaning of the word – unaligned with any institution except for the literary and artistic canon he so loves, and a thinker who comes to his own conclusions. [...]

This collection gives the reader a good sampling of Couteau's literary and scholarly talents, not the least of which are his interviews with writers he admires. Having spent many years as a journalist, I believe I have some ability to recognize and admire an artful interviewer, and Couteau is a master. His preparation is comprehensive, meticulous, and profound. His understanding of the process of writing in so many genres allows him insights into the particular problems faced by the writers he interviews. His style is conversational and relaxed, but deceptively so; he is always in control of the interview. This said, however, when a sudden fact or insight takes the interview down unexpected pathways, Couteau has the aesthetic nimbleness to recognize the opening and to follow it.

This collection features interviews with biographers, memoirists, historians, an inner-city antiviolence activist, and the creator of LSD. You'll also find herein Couteau's writings on literature, which I hesitate to call criticism since they lack the worst features of much literary criticism, which can be clogged with so much pretentiousness, cant, and philosophical obfuscation that it would take a plunger of Brobdingnagian proportions to restore a healthy flow. Couteau's essays are often rhapsodic appreciations and evocations of the work under study, and are stuffed with both insights and joy. Consider this, from the essay on Miller:

> And one of the great powers that surges forth from *Cancer* is the wit that explodes like a minefield beneath the reader when he least expects it. Again, at this stage of his career, since Miller had nothing to lose and only himself to please, he didn't give a rat's ass whether you'd be horrified, amused, or both. As is well known among the poor, humor is the one thing you cannot take away from a man who has been stripped of everything else. And humor is also the medium through which you will be reborn.

Couteau shares two things with Miller – love for Paris and birth in another place that crops up often in this collection, and which, as you would no doubt recognize, the moment Couteau (or Miller, for that matter), opened his mouth and spoke, as Brooklyn. Three of the pieces here are about a trinity of writers beloved by Couteau and closely associated with that famous borough – Walt Whitman, Henry Miller, and Hubert Selby. It is perhaps that each of these men shared in common an obsessive desire to produce something new and revolutionary with their words, something that was based not only on a powerful sense of self but also on closely observed and unflinching descriptions of their outer and the inner worlds in all their ugliness and wonder. Lucky for us, Couteau is doing much the same.

– An award-winning journalist and a professor of literature at Worcester Polytechnic Institute, James Dempsey is the author of *The Tortured Life of Scofield.*

Lightning Source UK Ltd.
Milton Keynes UK
UKHW011553170122
397285UK00002B/323

9 780996 688826